FAITH BUILDING

Daily Devotionals

31 devotionals to energize your faith

JERRY SAVELLE

FAITH BUILDING DAILY DEVOTIONALS
ISBN 1-888152-03-6

Unless otherwise stated, all Scripture quotations are
taken from *The King James Version* of the Bible.

Jerry Savelle Ministries International
P.O. Box 748
Crowley, TX 76036

THIS BOOK BELONGS TO:

....

....

....

Dear Friend,

I believe this daily devotional will encourage and inspire you in your personal walk with the Lord. I have carefully chosen 31 faith building lessons for you to read each day.

The devotionals are short enough for you to read in the morning, during lunch, or whenever you have free time, but packed with the Word of God to stir you up and keep your faith energized daily.

Each of the devotionals are a result of many years of studying God's Word, prayer, and fellowship with the Holy Spirit. It is so important that we build ourselves up in the Word of God, and learn to apply spiritual laws to EVERY situation we are facing - then we will not experience defeat, but we will be victorious in all that we set out to do!

I encourage you to read one devotional each day. After completing all 31, start with day one again, and review it over and over until it gets down into your spirit. You can also use this book as a daily Bible lesson to share with your friends and family. My prayer for you is to be blessed spiritually, mentally, physically, socially and financially as you continue your walk with the Lord.

In Him,

Dr. Jerry Savelle

CONTENTS

DAY   **PAGE**

1   Knowing God   11
2   Developing a Hunger and Thirst for God   15
3   Turn Your Ear Toward Heaven   19
4   Thinking On the Lord   23
5   Prayer - A Controlling Force   27
6   The Heartbeat of God is Souls   31
7   God is in Control   35
8   Hope - The Anchor of Your Soul   39
9   Leaving the Tears Behind   43
10 Weathering Life's Storms   47
11 Recovering from the Effects of Heat   51
12 God Will Turn Your Adversity Into Victory   55
13 In Time of Trouble...   59
14 If Satan Can't Steal Your Joy... He Can't Keep Your Goods   65
15 How to Guard Your Heart   69

DAY		PAGE

16	The Established Heart	73
17	A Right Mental Attitude	77
18	Rejoice! For This is the Will of God Concerning You	81
19	Are You Fed Up?	85
20	No Turning Back	89
21	Victory and Success are Yours	93
22	The Forces of Life	97
23	The Way of Faith	101
24	Faith for Today	105
25	Warnings and Admonitions from the Holy Spirit	109
26	Our Appointment with Destiny	113
27	Seven Steps to a Scriptural Foundation for Healing	117
28	Healing for Wounded Families	121
29	The Uncompromisingly Righteous	125
30	Abundantly Increasing in God's Divine Favor	129
31	You Are Somebody Special to God	133

KNOWING GOD

Many of God's people are struggling and can't seem to find out why nothing works for them anymore. Some are giving up and turning away. But for those who will remain faithful and determined to know their God, the best is yet to come. I believe that God wants to pour out His blessings; however, we must be in position to receive.

We read in Philippians of Paul's dedicated life toward God. Paul reveals his entire reason for existence was centered in Christ. Many Christians look at living the life of faith as a constant struggle, but Paul talks about a place in Christ where there is JOY in believing. I don't know about you, but if there's a place like that, I intend to get there.

Today's Scripture

That I may know him, and the power of his resurrection, and the fellowship of his sufferings, being made conformable unto his death.

Philippians 3:10

What is faith? Faith is nothing more than believing God. If you have faith in someone, that just simply means you trust them and have confidence in them. There is a place in God where it becomes JOYFUL to trust Him. If you were to say to some people, "Use your faith," they would groan, "Oh, has it come to that?" Where's the joy of believing? It's only through knowing God that you can truly understand what Paul meant.

When your motivation for studying the Bible is so that you can know Him and not just to find some "secret formula," then you will discover that your relationship will put you in a position to have your every need met. This is why Jesus said, "Seek ye first the kingdom of God..." or in other words, PUT GOD FIRST IN YOUR LIFE, then "...all these things shall be added unto you."

The revelation from the Word of God that reveals that God wants to bless us is certainly valid; however, some people have become selfish, self-centered, and have no desire to know God - they only want what He'll give them. Many people have never really entered into a "knowing" relationship with God. They know about Him, but they really don't **know** Him. Because they don't know Him, they tend to believe things about Him that are simply not true. Don't just look for some "get rich quick" scheme. Study the Word in order to know Him more intimately.

When you truly know someone, you know their likes and their dislikes. God knows you. He knows you so well that He has even numbered every hair on your head. He also knows the thought and intent of your heart. Now that's intimate.

I hear Christians say, "I don't know God's will." When you get to know Him, you'll know His will. That's the reason He wants you to know Him, so that He can reveal His will.

Many Christians can quickly identify the voice of the Devil, but then they say, "God never talks to me." How is it that they know the Devil's voice? Maybe they are spending too much time with the wrong *fellow*.

If my wife was to come into a room, and I didn't see her, I would be able to detect her voice when she started talking. Even with all the other voices, hers would become immediately apparent to me. Why? Because of intimate fellowship - union with each other. I know God because I spend time with Him. I know His voice because I've heard it often. When you really know Him, then it becomes a joy to trust Him. Get to know God today.

• •

DEVELOPING A HUNGER AND THIRST FOR GOD

Today's Scripture
• • • • • • • • • • • • • • • • • • •

O God, thou art my God; early will I seek thee: my soul thirsteth for thee, my flesh longeth for thee in a dry and thirsty land, where no water is.

Psalm 63:1

Are you dissatisfied on the inside? Do you feel like your spiritual walk has dried up? I have good news for you! I want to remind you of some things that will refresh your spiritual life.

In I Corinthians 15:1 *(Amplified Bible)*, the Apostle Paul is writing to born-again, spirit-filled believers, and he is saying that he needs to remind them of something. Many times we think we need for the minister to bring us a new revelation no one has ever heard. But we don't. We need to be reminded of the truths that have escaped us.

Verse one reads, *...it seems to have*

escaped you, brethren, of the Gospel (the glad tidings of salvation) which I proclaimed to you, which you welcomed and accepted and upon which your faith rests. Paul must have encountered the same situation because he is saying - **Hold on to what you have learned - remind yourself of it!** If it was necessary in his time, it's even more necessary for us.

Some Christians have the attitude, "I've heard it before..." or "I already know that." Faith comes by **hearing** and **hearing** by the Word of God. We need to be constantly refreshed in the Scriptures. If you have felt this way, you should realize you need to stir yourself up to continue in what you have learned.

The Holy Spirit keeps saying to me, "It's time for the Body of Christ to go BACK TO THE BASICS." When a building is being built, you don't destroy the foundation, you build on it. Jesus emphasized that if you try to build your life without a foundation, the first storm that comes along will bring great ruin.

It's very easy to become idle when you've heard it all, and you have access to so much. Here in America we have a "Word" church on every corner, thousands of tapes, books, and newsletters at our disposal and 24-hour Christian television. We are the most blessed generation that's ever lived! God is using every form of communication and media to get revelation into our lives, but we tend to try to live off of what we've heard instead of it being continually refreshed in us.

God responds to hunger. Jesus said, "When you are hungry and thirsty, you shall be filled." People sometimes say, "Well, I'm waiting on God to do this or that." God is waiting on you to get desperate for His power and His Spirit to move. He's waiting for you to get to the place where you are hungry and thirsty again to see His glory. When that happens, you will see His glory and power, and you will be filled! Don't live on yesterday's food. Continually feed your spirit with the Word of God!

TURN YOUR EAR TOWARD HEAVEN

You're hearing many voices, whether you realize it or not, it's true. Every moment of every day you're listening to someone. The voices of family, friends, newspapers, and television are speaking to you constantly. What they say can directly affect your life.

But, if you're a believer, you have another voice speaking to you as well. It's the voice of the Holy Spirit. The Holy Spirit has something to say about the days in which we live. I think we sometimes fail to give the Spirit of God credit for understanding our times. But He does. He knows what's coming in the future. He knows the solutions to the situations we're going to encounter. And if you and I are going to succeed in these last days, we must hear what He's saying. Even more, we

Today's Scripture

If any man have ears to hear, let him hear. And he said unto them, Take heed what ye hear: with what measure ye mete, it shall be measured to you: and unto you that hear shall more be given.

Mark 4:23-24

must believe His report!

We're living in a strange era. Even here in America, people are gripped with fear about the economy because of the many negative reports circulated by the media. They're afraid because they're listening to the wrong voices. This barrage of gloom and doom is designed by Satan to create panic and fear. And the bottom line is, it's aimed at getting Christians to stop giving.

You see, we were no threat to the Devil until we got a revelation of giving. As long as we were just the poor folks from the wrong side of the tracks playing church once a week, he didn't worry about us. But when we found out that giving connects us with the supernatural power of God, and enforces our covenant with Him in the earth, we suddenly became dangerous to the Devil.

No wonder we're constantly being bombarded with fear and negativity about the economy. The Devil knows that when we give, we prosper. When we prosper, we give more. So, he's trying to shut down the whole cycle with FEAR. He's trying to use fear to keep us from giving.

Yes, the voices of fear are speaking loudly today — but as believers, you and I must refuse to be moved by them. I'm not saying we should pretend a problem doesn't exist. Faith attacks that problem with the Word of God.

The real truth is that in the midst of a financial crisis, God's people can prosper as never before. Yes! Isaiah 60:2 says that when ...*darkness shall cover the earth, and gross darkness the people... the Lord shall arise upon thee, and his glory shall be seen upon thee.*

The Word says that when the world gets darker, the Church is going to get brighter. We don't have to go under with the world. And we don't have to listen to the voices in the media that say we do.

There is one voice, however, to which you do have to listen. The voice I'm talking about is your own. No voice on earth has a greater impact on your circumstances than YOUR OWN VOICE. It doesn't matter what you're going through today, the outcome of it will be determined by the words of your mouth.

What you allow your ears to hear, especially when it's coming out of your mouth, has a tremendous effect on your circumstances. Jesus taught about that in Mark 4. He said, *If any man have ears to hear, let him hear... Take heed what ye hear.* The

New International Version says, *Consider carefully what you hear.* The *Amplified Bible* says it this way, *Be careful what you are hearing.*

What are you hearing? To what voices are you listening? Are you filling your ears and your heart with the negative cries of the world, or the faith producing voice of the Word and the Holy Spirit? Your answer has a direct bearing on the circumstances of your life.

In Proverbs 8:34 *(Amplified Bible)*, God says, *Blessed is the man who listens to Me.* The Spirit is speaking. So turn your ear toward heaven. Tune out the voices of gloom and doom, and start using your own voice to get in agreement with what the Spirit is saying. Once you do that, it won't matter how shaky this world becomes, you'll be standing firm!

THINKING ON THE LORD

By Carolyn Savelle

Malachi 3:16 *(Amplified Bible)* says, *Then those who feared the Lord talked often one to another; and the Lord listened and heard it, and a book of remembrance was written before Him of those who reverenced and worshipfully feared the Lord and WHO THOUGHT ON HIS NAME.*

There is a book of remembrance written in heaven for those who talk about the Lord and think on His Name. When the Word is shared and the goodness of the Lord talked about and thought on, it is recorded in a book of remembrance.

All of us are tempted to think the wrong thoughts. However, if we will keep in mind that a book of remembrance is written in heaven, it will affect our thoughts. We should exercise a godly restraint where thoughts are concerned.

As Christians, Satan is our enemy, and he wants to defeat us. He doesn't want us to read the Word or hear the Word because he knows that knowledge will bring defeat for him. He wants to control our thought life.

It is in our thoughts that the battle begins. The thoughts come, but we must choose which thoughts to dwell on. We have to actively cast down the thoughts that are not in line with the Word of God.

Philippians 4:8 gives a wonderful frame of reference by which to judge our thoughts. Our instructions are to think on what is true, honest, just, pure, lovely, and of good report.

Proverbs 23:7 says, *...as he thinketh in his heart, so is he...* If you think negative thoughts and dwell on them, it will come to pass in your life. When thoughts of worldly temptations, fear, worry and insecurity come against your mind, cast down those imaginations and bring them into obedience to the Word of God. When you think on the Word of God, the strength of God, and the energizing power of the

Holy Spirit are at work within you.

It takes diligence to work on our minds. Our minds must line up with the Word of God in order for us to be successful in life. To think in line with the Word is to have the mind of Christ. Remember the Bible is our standard, guide, or frame of reference by which we judge our thoughts and actions. The Word of God is our final authority. I admonish you to THINK ON THE LORD!

PRAYER - A CONTROLLING FORCE

As you begin to study the ministry of Jesus, you will notice that prayer was a controlling force. Jesus spent much time in communication and fellowship with His Father through prayer; and as a result, there were miracles, signs, and wonders. In fact, Jesus was so aware of the power in prayer that He said in Luke 18:1, *...men ought always to pray, and not faint.* I particularly like the *Amplified* version: *...they ought always to pray and not to turn coward (faint, lose heart, and give up).*

I believe that Jesus is implying that prayer is designed to produce results. I heard one minister say, "Why should I worry when I can pray!" This should be our attitude in prayer. I pray not because it's the religious

And it came to pass in those days, that he went out into a mountain to pray, and continued all night in prayer to God.

Luke 6:12

•••

thing to do, but to gain results.

Prayer should be a prevailing factor in the life of every believer. The people who most powerfully affect the lives of others are those who spend time in prayer. One very famous preacher expressed it in this statement: "Before you can talk well to men about God, you must first be able to talk well to God about men."

I am convinced that in order for believers to fully illustrate Jesus in their lives, they must learn how to build an accurate prayer life. As an aid, I would like to share with you a few major points that have been beneficial to me in learning how to pray accurately. I trust that these points will be helpful to you and prayer will become a controlling force in your life.

1.   **Make God's Word "His" part of your prayer life.** The Word is our contract with God, and His contract with us.

2.   **Base your prayer on the answer found in God's Word.** The Word covers the entire spectrum of human existence. Always remember to hold fast to the "answer" to your problem and not to the problem.

3. **Go boldly to the throne of grace and obtain.** You have the right to stand in the presence of God without a sense of fear.

4. **Lean hard on your rightstanding with God.** You are the righteousness of God, and your prayers will avail.

5. **Pray to the Father in the Name of Jesus.** Remember that the Name of Jesus gets the ear of God, and we have been given the power of attorney to use that Name.

6. **Realize that you can ask what you will.** God's Word is His will. When His Word is abiding in you, then His will and your will become the same.

7. **Recognize with whom you are wrestling.** Spiritual warfare takes place in prayer; therefore, you must put on the whole armor of God.

8. **Believe you receive when you pray.** Walk by faith and not by sight. Don't be moved by adverse circumstances.

9. **Keep yourself free from strife and unforgiveness.** Realize that faith will

not work in an unforgiving heart.

10. **Give praise for the victory.** Praise will stop the enemy and open the door to the greater blessings of God.

Notice the affect of prayer as a controlling factor in Luke 6:12-19 and Mark 6:46-56. Put prayer to work for you today!

THE HEARTBEAT OF GOD IS SOULS
By Carolyn Savelle

We know Jesus is coming soon. Signs of His soon appearing are all around us. Now is not the time to be caught off-guard. It's time to get prepared!

Matthew 24:34-35 says, *Verily I say unto you, this generation shall not pass, till all these things be fulfilled. Heaven and earth shall pass away, but my words shall not pass away.*

These Scriptures refer to Israel becoming a nation and that occurred in 1948. Jesus is saying that the generation that sees this come to pass is the generation that will not pass away. This is the most exciting time to be alive! God has privileged us to live in this time. We are the generation that will see the return of the

Today's Scripture

That ye may walk honestly toward them that are without, and that ye may have lack of nothing.

I Thessalonians 4:12

Lord Jesus Christ.

Matthew 24:42-47 *(Living Bible)* states, *So be prepared, for you don't know what day your Lord is coming. Just as a man can prevent trouble from thieves by keeping watch for them, so you can avoid trouble by always being ready for my unannounced return. Are you a wise and faithful servant of the Lord? Have I given you the task of managing my household, to feed my children day by day? Blessings on you if I return and find you faithfully doing your work. I will put such faithful ones in charge of everything I own!*

My priorities have changed because I know that Jesus is coming so soon. Some of the things that were so important to me before aren't important now. I don't want to use my precious faith and energy on just material things. They're not important. I want to apply all my faith to winning souls and taking as many as possible to heaven with me. When you make winning souls your first priority, all of your needs will be met!

Winning the lost is the very heartbeat of God. All of His plans and purposes from the beginning of time up to this very hour have centered on man's redemption. We must be at work to fulfill the vision of winning the lost, feeding the sheep, and making disciples of new converts. If we're faithful to this commission, and con-

tinue to stand firm in the faith, we will soon hear Him say, "Well done, thou good
and faithful servant."

GOD IS IN CONTROL

These are exciting times! We are seeing the words of the prophets fulfilled right before our eyes! Truly we are living in the last days!

We must begin to live each day as though Jesus is coming back before morning. That's the reason the early Church was such a powerful Church. Jesus told them that He would return in the same manner that they saw Him leave and they were to occupy until He returned. He instructed them to preach to the uttermost parts of the earth, heal the sick, raise the dead, and cast out devils. They didn't know exactly when He was coming back, so they acted as though it might be any day.

In Acts 3 it says that heaven is holding Jesus back until the restitution of all things.

Today's Scripture

...Yet once, it is a little while, and I will shake the heavens, and the earth, and the sea, and the dry land; And I will shake all nations, and the desire of all nations shall come: and I will fill this house with glory, saith the Lord of hosts. The silver is mine, and the gold is mine, saith the Lord of hosts.

Haggai 2:6-8

The Holy Spirit is at work in the earth right now setting the stage for this glorious event. In these days, it is imperative for us to be established in the Word of God. There are many voices in the world today trying to deceive. There are those who are messengers of Satan and are leading people astray. The Bible says that in the last days many will fall for doctrines of devils (I Timothy 4:1). That's the reason you owe it to yourself to become so established in God's Word that you can't be seduced.

Spiritual battles have been won, but the war is not over. We must continue to come against the strongholds of Satan and fight the good fight of faith. No matter what it looks like in the natural, GOD IS IN CONTROL! I don't intend to "blow it" when the greatest event in the entire history of the Church is about to take place!

We need to know what the Word of God says about these situations happening in our world instead of falling for what the press says about it. The walls of Jericho fell, and the walls of Berlin fell also. God is moving, setting everything in order to fulfill Bible prophecy. You can't keep God from doing what He said He would do!

We must get stirred up! Time is running out! We have the promise of His glorious appearing! When the earth is covered with darkness, the glory of the Lord shall be seen upon us. God is going to raise up a glorious Church in the midst of the darkest hour the world has ever seen! HE IS IN CONTROL!

HOPE: THE ANCHOR OF YOUR
SOUL - By Carolyn Savelle

Many people use the word *"hope"* just as they do the word "wish." It is much greater than that. What is *hope*? The dictionary tells us that *hope* is *a yearning with expectation or anticipation.* The Greek definition of *hope* means *to be intensely expectant, to be confidently looking forward to something you fully expect to happen.*

Do you desire something in your life? Do you desire to have your whole household saved? Do you desire to be out of debt, and to help meet the needs of others and give into the work of God? That hope or anticipation can be the anchor of your soul. Hope helps you set divinely-inspired goals.

Today's Scripture

Blessed is the man that trusteth in the Lord, and whose hope the Lord is.

Jeremiah 17:7

What is the meaning for the word *anchor*? *Anchor* is defined as *something that serves to hold an object firmly in place.* An anchor keeps you from drifting. Hope can keep your soul, which is made up of your mind, will, emotions, and thinking faculties, at rest in turbulent waters. When the waves are crashing against your ship, and you're in the middle of the storm, the anchor of hope serves its purpose by keeping you at rest. That hope keeps you from drifting off into troubled waters.

We experience the greatest battle in our **mind**. When you have prayed and believed God for certain things, and your head starts telling you there's no way this is going to happen, HOPE is the expectation that will anchor your soul and straighten up your thinking. Hope will keep you at rest, firm and steady, when your mind is being bombarded by thoughts of giving up.

David says in Psalm 42:4-11 *(Living Bible), Take courage, my soul! Do you remember those times (but how could you ever forget them!)... singing with joy, praising the Lord? Why then be downcast? Why be discouraged and sad? ...but I will meditate upon your kindness... But O my soul, don't be discouraged. Don't be upset. Expect God to act!...*

Don't forget all those times God answered your prayers and performed miracles in your life. Remembering those impossible situations He brought you out of will cause hope to rise up on the inside of you and anchor your soul!

You have to make your mind, will, emotions, and thinking faculties line-up with what the Word of God says. You have to **tell** your soul to have hope, to not give up, and to trust God!

What does *hopeless* mean? The dictionary defines *hopeless* as: *despondent, void of hope, and despair.* Have you ever seen anyone in total despair? All thought of changing is gone, and they can't even imagine their life being different. *Hopeless* means *incurable, or irreparable.* But, thank God, we have the "giver of hope" on the inside of us. As long as you have hope in God, you have an anchor for your soul.

Romans 15:4 says, *For whatsoever things were written aforetime were written for our learning, that we through patience and comfort of the scriptures might have hope.* The Scriptures give you **comfort**, **hope**, and **rest**. You must dwell on what God says about your circumstances.

Faith is calm assurance that God will completely take care of you and meet your every need. Your mind, will, emotions, and thinking faculties shall rest in expectancy, anticipation, and in the desire that God has for you.

Whatever situation you're in, know that the Word of God has been written for your learning and your comfort. The Scriptures will be soothing to your mind. Whatever it is that you're desiring: financial break-through, healing, loved ones saved, you are to abound in hope. We need to expect these things to happen in our lives.

Hope is a vital ingredient. You must have it. In every situation, you need to go to the Word of God. It's your reference, your guide by which you judge everything. The Word of God has an answer to it, and that Word will bring comfort to you in every situation in your life and will cause you to become alive!

LEAVING THE TEARS BEHIND

If you don't know exactly what the "Valley of Baca" is, you can read about it in Psalm 84. It's a phrase that means a place of "weeping or misery." A place of crisis and pain. An emotional desert where the dry winds of disappointment constantly blow.

It's a place all of us eventually go. All of us... even faith-filled, Holy Spirit-baptized believers. Somebody may say, "Yes, Brother Jerry, God creates those painful places to help us grow." No, He doesn't. The Devil, not God, is the one who brings misery. He's the one who comes to kill, steal, and destroy. And that's exactly why he designs those *Valleys of Baca* - to destroy us. All too often he succeeds.

That's right. Many believers don't

Today's Scripture

For the Lord God is a sun and shield: the Lord will give grace and glory: no good thing will he withhold from them that walk uprightly.

Psalm 84:11

make it through the Valley of Baca. They go in there, suffer setbacks, and disappointments, and are never heard from again. They give up hope and allow misery to become their permanent dwelling place.

But I'm here to tell you that's not how the Word of God tells us it should be! Psalm 84:5-6 says, *Blessed is the man whose strength is in God... Who **passing through** the valley of Baca..."* Did you notice the last phrase? ***Passing through the Valley of Baca***. Passing through! The valley of misery or weeping is not meant to be a permanent dwelling place. It's simply a place the people of God occasionally pass through.

You've got to remember that! Baca doesn't last forever. So don't lay down your faith and die when you get there. No! Stand up and say, "This is not where I live. This is not God's best for me. I'm just passing through!"

Here's something else you need to know about Baca. It can be a place of blessings! Psalm 84:6-7 *(Amplified Bible)* says those who trust in God while *Passing through the Valley of Weeping (Baca), they make it a place of springs; the early rain also fills [the pools] with blessings. They go from strength to strength [increasing in victorious power]...* There are blessings for you in *Baca* if you'll trust God as you pass through it. What's more, you can come out on the other side stronger than you've ever been before!

If you'll stand on the Word, that battle with sickness, that financial trouble, that time of misery the Devil puts you through, will just give you another story to tell about how powerful God is. You can come out of Baca so full of faith and rejoicing that the Devil will be sorry he ever messed with you.

You're going to find an abundance of people, most of them sincere Christian people, who are eager to convince you that there is no help for you in God. The question is: How are you going to respond to it? Are you going to hang your head and agree with it? Are you going to say, "Well, I guess you're right. I guess I just better learn to live with this misery. After all, it looks like it's here to stay?"

If you'll notice, the psalmist David knew what it was like to go through Baca. He said, *Many are they that say of my soul, there is no help for him in God. BUT THOU, O LORD, ART A SHIELD FOR ME; MY GLORY, AND THE LIFTER OF MY HEAD!*

There were many times when David was in such deep misery that he couldn't help talking about it. But his psalms never end with misery. No, before it's over, he always starts talking about his covenant with God. He always starts talking faith.

Next time you're in Baca, you need to ask God the same thing David did. You need to say, "God, shall I just take this sitting down? Shall I just sit here and die? Do I just sit here when the enemy has invaded my home and let him carry off my family, my health, and my money?" If you do, God will tell you just what He told David every time. He'll say, "Pursue!"

When you're in pain and misery, don't sit there until you die. Get up and be aggressive. Take charge! Do what David did and encourage yourself and strengthen yourself in the Lord your God.

Go back in there and listen to those faith tapes again. Get your Bible out and start reading again. Get yourself to church and let somebody preach to you. Encourage yourself! Don't wait for somebody to come along with a special anointing for encouragement. Encourage yourself! PURSUE and you shall surely overtake them, and without fail, recover all!

WEATHERING LIFE'S STORMS

When the storms of life strike, it's what happens **in** you that will determine what happens **to** you. At the first sign of a storm, remain calm and maintain your trust and confidence in God's ability to see you through to victory.

Here are some comforting facts you should know about rough weather:

1. **Rough weather doesn't last forever.** II Corinthians 4:17-18 says *...our light affliction, which is but for a moment... the things which are seen are temporal...*

2. **Rough weather will try to wear you down, but don't let**

Today's Scripture

Peace I leave with you, my peace I give unto you: not as the world giveth, give I unto you. Let not your heart be troubled, neither let it be afraid.

John 14:27

it wear you out. Acts 27:20 says, *And when neither sun nor stars in many days appeared, and no small tempest lay on us, all hope that we should be saved was then taken away.*

3. **Rough weather can cause you to lose your sense of direction.** Hebrews 12:1-2 *(New American Standard)* says *...Let us also lay aside every encumbrance, and the sin which so easily entangles us, and let us run with endurance the race that is set before us, **fixing our eyes on Jesus...***

4. **Rough weather can bring upon you an overwhelming sense of failure.** Mark 4:38 says *...Carest thou not that we perish?*

5. **Your attitude about rough weather can either make you or break you.** Proverbs 23:7 *(New American Standard)* says, *as he thinks within himself, so he is.*

Let me encourage you to strengthen yourself and don't let the enemy steal the Word out of your heart. No matter what you are facing now, God is able to see you to the other side victoriously. When I experience the storms of life, I've found that it's important to remember that:

- Defeat comes from looking back;
- Distraction comes from looking around;
- Discouragement comes from looking down; and
- Deliverance comes from looking up.

God is on your side and will enable you to be victorious **in** and **through** your storm!

RECOVERING FROM THE EFFECTS OF HEAT

In II Timothy 3:1 *(Amplified Bible)*, Paul tells us, *But understand this, that in the last days will come (set in) perilous times of great stress and trouble [hard to deal with and hard to bear].*

Some of God's people are on the verge of giving up because their troubles have become too "hard to deal with." In times like this, you either stand on what you've learned, or you give up. There is no neutral place. NOW is the most opportune time to stand on the Word of God.

Have you had situations lately that have been hard to deal with? We all have! However, let me share something with you about, "heat waves and fiery trials." THEY

Today's Scripture

Beloved, think it not strange concerning the fiery trials which is to try you, as though some strange thing happened unto you: But rejoice, inasmuch as ye are partakers of Christ's suffering; that, when his glory shall be revealed, ye may be glad also with exceeding joy.

I Peter 4:12-13

ARE SEASONAL! They don't last forever! It's what you do IN those perilous times that will determine how quickly you get OUT of them.

You must not let go of what you have learned because that is the very thing that will put you over. If you let go of what you've learned, God doesn't have an avenue through which to work. You must remain stable in these unstable times through your faith in God. Some have said the "message of faith" is not the message of the hour, but I personally believe that it's never been more needed than right now! **The just shall live by faith**!

In these perilous times, don't be deceived into giving up because you don't understand why all this is happening to you. I Peter 4:12 *(Amplified Bible)* clearly states, *Beloved, do not be amazed and bewildered at the fiery ordeal which is taking place to test your quality, as though something strange (unusual and alien to you and your position) were befalling you.* The *New International Version* says, *...do not be surprised at the painful trial you are suffering...*

Notice, Peter said that you shouldn't be surprised when your uncompromising position or stand on the Word comes under attack. Knowing that perilous times are coming will help you to be prepared when they do come. Some are bewildered and disillusioned because of the trial they are experiencing, saying, *"Why is this happening to me? I don't understand why this is happening to me."* The Devil can defeat you while you are thinking that. He loves for you to ask questions like these and open the door to discouragement.

When you are going through fiery trials, don't think it is strange that the Devil is trying to steal the Word from your heart. He knows you will win if you stay in faith and stand on the Word of God. If you are experiencing a fiery trial, then you are a candidate for a time of refreshing. God wants you to recover from the effects of heat and continue to be fruitful and productive.

If you are going to experience a time of refreshing, you will have to be where the refreshing is - in the presence of the Lord. You won't experience a refreshing running **from** God - you must run **to** God. In His presence is fullness of joy. God calls a *time of refreshing*: **Recovering from the effects of heat!**

Let me pray for you right now: Father, in the mighty Name of Jesus, I pray for each one reading this devotion, who realizes their need for a refreshing. I pray that as they spend time in the presence of the Lord, a wonderful refreshing will come on them. This refreshing will wash away all the hurts, disappointments and scorching from the effects of heat and fiery trials. Then the cool breezes of the Holy Spirit will bring wholeness, soundness, and life to every part of their lives, in Jesus' Name. Amen!

GOD WILL TURN YOUR ADVERSITY INTO VICTORY

Today's Scripture

II Corinthians 2:14 says, *Now thanks be unto God, which* **always** *causeth us to triumph in Christ, and maketh manifest the savor of his knowledge by us in every place.* The key word here is **always**. That gets rid of the philosophy, "win a few, lose a few." *...Always causeth us to triumph in Christ.* However, it does not say that we'll never be under attack; nor does it say that we'll never have adversity.

Somebody might say, "I haven't always triumphed." Well, that's not God's fault. Because Paul says, God ALWAYS causes us to triumph. In the mind of God, victory belongs to you. No matter what kind of persecution, adversity, or attack you may be under, in the mind of God, the end result is triumph!

Now thanks be unto God, which always causeth us to triumph in Christ, and maketh manifest the savour of his knowledge by us in every place.

II Corinthians 2:14

You can give up before victory comes. You can get weary in well-doing before victory comes. You can get discouraged and quit before victory comes, but I am totally convinced that with every attack that Satan launches against us, God already has a victory in mind!

What you do *during* the attack will determine whether or not you *triumph*! I made up my mind years ago that I'm not going to accept failure. I didn't say I've never had opportunity to fail, or that I've never had a setback. I have had many opportunities to fail. But it's not over until God has an opportunity to turn it into a triumph!

I don't know what you're going through today, but I do know this: you have the potential to experience a triumph, IF YOU WON'T GIVE UP! The greater the attack, the greater the potential for a great victory. I don't know why we want to give up when God's already given us all the incentive we need to continue in faith.

For those who remain faithful, God will turn every setback into a triumph, and every stumbling block into a stepping stone to victory! Don't give up! God is a Master at turning every bad thing that Satan launches against you into an instrument of victory! The Bible even tells us that He'll turn every curse into a blessing.

Deuteronomy 30:3, 7 says, *That then the Lord thy God will turn thy captivity, and have compassion upon thee... And the Lord thy God will put all these curses upon thine enemies, and on them that hate thee, which persecuted thee.* God says that He'll take the curses off of you and put them on your enemies. Not only will God turn your captivity, but He will bring you into a new place of dominion.

He says, if you'll be faithful; if you'll serve Him with all of your heart and all of your soul; if you'll not give up under pressure; not give up because it looks like God is not doing anything, **then** He'll be faithful to you.

What looks to be a total disaster, God can turn into a wonderful victory. He can turn all those tears of sorrow into tears of joy. God can put joy in your heart **during** your adversity. You can get to the point where you laugh at the Devil in every attack because **he is defeated**! The Bible says that a merry heart doeth good like a medicine.

You know that's got to be a slap in the Devil's face when he's plotted and planned for months to set you up for the kill, expecting you to be filled with grief and sorrow, and wanting to quit, and the first thing you do is get up and start dancing before the Lord.

The Devil has already made a trophy with **your** name on it, thinking he will defeat you, but when you come at him with **patience**, the **Word** of God, and the **joy** of the Lord, he has to immediately forfeit that trophy because it belongs to you and God! Don't let the Devil win, take it as your own victory to add to your trophy case!

I don't know what kind of trial you're going through today, but if you'll be patient in it, then you will see the end of the Lord - compassion and mercy. God is going to turn this thing in your life into a victory! God can use the **very thing** that Satan has brought against you as a tool for deliverance and victory. In the natural, it may look like total disaster, but God can turn it into the greatest blessing you have ever experienced.

Choose to continue to stand because we have everything to gain by standing, and everything to lose by quitting. Why give up? Why quit believing the Word? The Word works!

IN TIME OF TROUBLE...

Recently, as I was reading Psalm 27, the Lord said to me, "I'm going to give you a checklist for what to do in time of trouble. It worked for David, and it will work for you." The Psalmist, David, had faced trouble many times in his life but always found God to be more than enough to see him through and to cause him to become the victor in every case.

This checklist has been such a blessing to me that I sensed in my heart it would be beneficial to you. It comes right out of the Word of God, and I, for one, know that it will produce results. Follow it closely, study and meditate the Scripture references and then use it at the very first sign of trouble.

Today's Scripture

For in the time of trouble he shall hide me in his pavilion: in the secret of his tabernacle shall he hide me; he shall set me up upon a rock.

Psalm 27:5

1. **Realize that God is your light**.

   The Lord is my light... Psalm 27:1

   God is our wisdom, knowledge, and understanding. James 1:5 says, *If any of you lack wisdom, let him ask of God, that giveth to all men liberally, and upbraideth not; and it shall be given him.* Don't lean to carnal reasoning!

2. **Realize that God is your salvation**.

   The Lord is my light and my salvation... Psalm 27:1

   The word *salvation* implies: safety, health, prosperity, deliverance, and soundness. Salvation comes on the wings of confession. Romans 10:10 says, *For with the heart man believeth unto righteousness; and with the mouth confession is made unto salvation.*

3. **Realize that God is your strength**.

   The Lord is my light and my salvation... the Lord is the strength of my life...

Psalm 27:1

Philippians 4:13 says, *I can do all things through Christ which strengtheneth me.*

4. **Keep your heart free from fear**.

...whom shall I fear ...of whom shall I be afraid? Psalm 27:1

Fear activates Satan, just as faith activates God. II Timothy 1:7 says, *For God hath not given us a spirit of fear; but of power, and of love, and of a sound mind.*

5. **Don't cast away your confidence**.

...though war should rise against me, in this will I be confident. Psalm 27:3

Hebrews 10:35-36 says, *Cast not away therefore your confidence, which hath great recompense of reward. For ye have need of patience, that, after ye have done the will of God, ye might receive the promise.* Don't give up, the victory is coming!

6.   **Resist the temptation to become oppressed**.

Though an host encamp against me, my heart shall not fear... And now shall mine head be lifted up above mine enemies round about me... Psalm 27:3,6

Isaiah 54:14 says, *In righteousness shalt thou be established: thou shalt be far from oppression; for thou shalt not fear: and from terror; for it shall not come near thee.*

7.   **Offer sacrifices of joy**.

...therefore will I offer in his tabernacle sacrifices of joy... Psalm 27:6

If Satan can rob you of your joy, he can rob you of your strength also. Nehemiah 8:10 says, *...for the JOY of the Lord is your STRENGTH.*

8.   **Seek God's face - stay in His presence**.

When thou saidst, Seek ye my face; my heart said unto thee, Thy face, Lord, will I seek. Psalm 27:8.

Psalm 16:11 says, *Thou wilt shew me the path of life: in thy presence is fulness of joy; at thy right hand there are pleasures forevermore.*

9. **Faint not, but believe to see His goodness**.

   I had fainted, unless I had believed to see the goodness of the Lord in the land of the living. Psalm 27:13.

10. WAIT ON THE LORD AND BE OF GOOD COURAGE.

   Wait on the Lord: be of good courage, and He shall strengthen thine heart: wait, I say, on the Lord. Psalm 27:14.

   Wait means *to minister unto.* The Bible tells us in Isaiah 40:31, *But they that wait upon the Lord shall renew their strength; they shall mount up with wings as eagles; they shall run, and not be weary; and they shall walk, and not faint.* The Bible encourages believers to keep looking up, maintain joy, don't be distracted or discouraged. God is on our side, and He will see us through to VICTORY!

IF SATAN CAN'T STEAL YOUR JOY...
HE CAN'T KEEP YOUR GOODS!

Today's Scripture

II Corinthians 4:8,9 says, *We are troubled on every side, yet not distressed; we are perplexed, but not in despair; persecuted, but not forsaken; cast down, but not destroyed.* A lot of people read it this way: "We are troubled, we are perplexed, we are persecuted, we are cast down - oh, woe is us." That's not what Paul said. He always leaves it on a note of victory!

The Apostle Paul says in one translation, *I might get knocked down, but you're never going to knock me out!* There's a difference in being knocked down and knocked out. I've been knocked down a few times, but when I fall, the most natural thing in the world to do is GET UP!

Then he said unto them, Go your way, eat the fat, and drink the sweet, and send portions unto them for whom nothing is prepared: for this day is holy unto our Lord: neither be ye sorry; for the joy of the Lord is your strength.

Nehemiah 8:10

Jesus said very clearly that Satan comes immediately to steal the Word. How? Through affliction, persecution, the cares of this world, the lust of other things, and the deceitfulness of riches. What is the Devil trying to steal from us? THE WORD.

Why is it so important for the Devil to steal the Word? God's Word produces **joy** in our hearts. When we read the Word and realize that it's God's will for us to prosper and be in health, that produces **joy** on the inside of us.

Nehemiah 8:10 says, *The **joy** of the Lord is your **strength**.* Satan is after your joy. He especially likes to use the "little things" to steal our joy, such as: your car won't start, your hair isn't looking right, a husband and wife start fussing... The Devil knows that if he can get your joy, even over something "little," he can steal your strength. If you have no strength, you can't resist the Devil. If you can't resist the Devil, he won't flee.

Did you know that the number one way he tries to get the Word out of you is through stealing some material thing from you? He can't just reach in and get your joy out of your heart. He has to work in this "material realm" to try to get something spiritual out of you. Joy is a spiritual force.

Hebrews 10:34 says, *For ye had compassion of me in my bonds, and took joyfully the spoiling of your goods.* The Lord showed me this Scripture one night, and I began to really notice what it was saying. Then the Lord said to me, "Son, if the Devil can't steal your joy, he can't keep your goods."

Have you ever had the Devil steal something from you? Do you know that it was the Devil who stole your car, your money, or whatever it was? God is not saying to lift your hands and praise the Lord because something was stolen from you. He is saying that you must maintain your joy. Don't let the Devil get your joy.

When you know the Devil has stolen something from you, it is very easy to get discouraged and allow your joy to depart from you. Right at that moment, when you don't have any joy, you have no resistance to the attack. But, it doesn't have to be that way. If he can't get your joy, **he can't keep what he stole from you**!

Do you want it back? Jeremiah 33:11 says, *The voice of joy, and the voice of gladness, and the voice of the bridegroom, and the voice of the bride, and the voice of them that shall say, Praise the Lord of hosts: for the Lord is good; for His mercy endureth for ever: and of them that shall bring the SACRIFICE OF PRAISE into the house of the Lord. For I will cause to return the captivity of the land, as at the first, saith the Lord.*

When would praise be a sacrifice? When you don't feel like it! When the Devil has just attacked you! But God is saying, IF *you'll maintain joy no matter what the Devil brings against you, I'll return your goods!* (Author's paraphrase) Praise God!

And it even gets better than that! Proverbs 6:31 says, *But if he* (the thief) *be found, he shall restore sevenfold; he shall give all the substance of his house.* God is saying, "I'll not only get it back to you, I'll make him pay it back seven times!"   That is, if we don't let the Devil get our joy.

So, I encourage you, don't let the Devil defeat you by stealing your joy. Remember, that when you have no joy, you have no strength, and that's when Satan can come in and rob you of everything you have. Satan has no refuge when JOY is present. THE JOY OF THE LORD IS YOUR STRENGTH!

HOW TO GUARD YOUR HEART

Today's Scripture

And these are they which are sown on good ground; such as hear the word, and receive it, and bring forth fruit, some thirtyfold, some sixty and some an hundred.

Mark 4:20

We are to guard our hearts with all diligence, for out of our hearts come the forces of life. The Devil is continually seeking entrance into our hearts through hurt feelings, strife, bitterness, anger, and offense. Study these steps I've listed on HOW TO GUARD YOUR HEART:

1. **Don't let the sun go down on your wrath**.

    Be ye angry, and sin not: let not the sun go down upon your wrath: Neither give place to the devil.

    Ephesians 4:26-27

    We are not to let a day go by without cleansing our hearts and getting rid of all anger, irritation, and offense. This includes offense against anyone and everyone - no matter how mean or hateful they are. The Bible is giving us clear instruction here. You may get angry with someone, but little stones of offense in our hearts soon can become big stumbling blocks to the flow of the power of God. *Your faith will not work when you fail to walk in love.*

2.   **Hold your tongue; don't give way to anger**

If thou hast done foolishly in lifting up thyself, or if thou hast thought evil, lay thine hand upon thy mouth.

Proverbs 30:32

Several times a day, you may be tempted to "give someone a piece of your mind." Proverbs 16:32 says, *He that is slow to anger is better than the mighty; and he that ruleth his spirit than he that taketh a city.* In God's eyes, when you begin to rule your spirit instead of just giving way to anger and bad temper, you are mightier than the man who wins a battle and takes a city.

Now go before God in prayer and pray out whatever has come against your heart. When you are praying earnestly for someone who is trying your patience, you will fall in love with them. It is impossible to be angry with a brother and be asking God to bless them at the same time.

3. **Pray I Corinthians 13:4-8 from The Amplified Bible daily.**

Love endures long and is patient and kind; love never is envious nor boils over with jealousy, is not boastful or vainglorious, does not display itself haughtily. It is not conceited (arrogant and inflated with pride); it is not rude (unmannerly) and does not act unbecomingly. Love (God's love in us) does not insist on its own rights or its own way, for it is not self-seeking; it is not touchy or fretful or resentful; it takes no account of the evil done to it (it pays no attention to a suffered wrong).

It does not rejoice at injustice and unrighteousness, but rejoices when right and truth prevail. Love bears up under anything and everything that comes, is ever ready to believe the best of every person, its hopes are fadeless under all circumstances and it endures everything (without weakening). Love never fails, (never fades out or becomes obsolete or comes to an end)...

This is the God-kind of love that is in your heart because Jesus lives in you. It is one of the fruit of the Spirit. The love of God that is shed abroad in your heart will be a guard and protection when Satan tries to gain a foothold.

4.   **Pray in the Spirit (tongues) daily**.

But ye, beloved, building up yourselves on your most holy faith, praying in the Holy Ghost, keep yourselves in the love of God, looking for the mercy of our Lord Jesus Christ unto eternal life. Jude 20-21.

Praying in the Holy Spirit causes you to make progress in the things of God. You will grow much more quickly and be much stronger as you release your prayer language. The Holy Spirit will garrison round about you and mount guard in your heart as you continuously offer prayers to God in faith.

THE ESTABLISHED HEART

The time in which we live today offers us ample opportunity to be troubled, to be afraid, to be easily shaken by bad news. The newscasts are filled with it. You can look at the trouble, listen to the bad news, and talk about it to other people; but you are only magnifying the works of the Devil. The Bible says that where sin abounds, grace does much more abound (Romans 5:20). Today, we are in the perfect position to have the grace of God manifested at its absolute greatest.

Psalm 112 is the description of a man who has his heart established in God's Word. He is not afraid of evil tidings; he is not afraid of bad news; he is not moved by contradictory evidence; he is not moved by the woes and cares and pressures of this world. His heart is

Today's Scripture

He shall not be afraid of evil tidings: his heart is fixed, trusting in the Lord.

Psalm 112:7

•••

fixed and settled trusting in the Lord.

You must realize one very important fact: the believer can live today in the midst of all the turmoil and the pressures in the world without being shaken by them. You can live with your heart established, trusting in the Lord, and not be afraid of anything Satan can bring upon the earth.

In order to have your heart established in God's Word, you must reach the point where you are not moved by anything - not by what you hear, nor by what you see, nor by what you feel. The established heart knows that in every situation, God is more than enough, and He will meet his every need according to His riches in glory by Christ Jesus. I am convinced that this is the intention of the Father God to every believer.

The established heart trusts in the Lord. If you expect to trust in the Lord, you must trust His Word because God and His Word are one and the same. You will never be able to have your heart established except by the Word of God. It takes God's Word to get the job done.

Find out what the Apostle Paul learned in the New Testament and you, too, can stand in the midst of Satan, demons, sickness, disease, and even death itself and say, "I am persuaded that nothing can separate me from the love of Christ. I am more than a conqueror in all these things!" Paul was established in the Word, and it made him able to stand victoriously, more than a conqueror!

I am not implying that living by faith and getting your heart established in God's Word is easy. Satan will not simply lay down and let you get grounded in the Word. He will do his best to stop it. But don't be discouraged. The more Word you get into your spirit, the stronger you will grow. It is to your advantage to become settled and fixed on the Word so that the floods and storms of life will not shake you.

The reason so many Christians are being robbed of the blessings of God is because they have failed to get God's Word established in their hearts. If you pray according to God's Word and follow the instructions outlined there, you **will** get results. If you miss it, then it is your fault, not God's.

Read Isaiah 26:3 and I Peter 1:13 for examples of believers whose hearts were established in God's Word.

A RIGHT MENTAL ATTITUDE

There are many aspects involved in living the life of faith and one of them is maintaining a right mental attitude. Do you believe God is an all-knowing God? Hebrews 4:13 tells us that everything we do is open and naked unto the eyes of Him with Whom we have to do. There is nothing hidden from God. It also tells us that He is able to discern the thought and intent of our heart. He wouldn't be God if He didn't know those things. He's an all-knowing God.

The Bible tells us that He even knows your need before you ask. You're not kidding God when you make Him promises you don't intend to fulfill. When I was a young boy growing up, I made Him promises that I would serve Him if He would do certain things. And

Today's Scripture

Thou wilt keep him in perfect peace, whose mind is stayed on thee: because he trusteth in thee.

Isaiah 26:3

He would always come through and do His part, but I didn't keep my end of the bargain.

God knows everything about you. However, there is a fellow who doesn't know you that well. His name is Satan. Somebody asks, "Does Satan know my thoughts?" He does not. The only thing he knows about you is what *influences* you and what you *yield* to. Someone may ask, "Can he read my mind?" No, only the thoughts that you allow him to place there.

Satan does not know you like God knows you. The only way he can find out about how you will react is to test you in different situations. He's got an experiment going on with you.

The Bible tells us that God has recorded every idle word that comes out of our mouth. Satan, too, has a little messenger who records all of our words and actions. His messenger then reports back to headquarters, and Satan learns about you through your actions. For instance, let's say that I am being tested by the Devil where sickness is concerned. I have these symptoms in my body, and I will either talk the Word or talk the problem. Now, if I say, "Oh, dear God, I'm going to die," then Satan's messenger reports back, "Every time he gets a symptom, he talks death. That's good - he's snared by the words of his mouth. We can use that, master."

Remember, words are vehicles or carriers. They'll bring success or failure. They bring life or death. Proverbs 18:21 says, *Death and life are in the power of the tongue...* We must begin to speak positive confessions, and then the next time Satan's messenger comes back for an attack, we'll blow him away with, "Thus saith the Lord, it is written..." And his messenger will run back and say, "Something happened, boss. He changed while I was away."

Winning is easy. It's the talking yourself into winning that's difficult. Remember, out of the abundance of the heart, the mouth speaketh. You're not going to be able to talk positive if your heart is full of negative things.

It's your decision to have a right mental attitude about life's circumstances. Remember that God's Word is the foundation of a right mental attitude. Study these principles and allow them to get on the inside of you:

1.   A right mental attitude is more than wishful thinking. It is actually facing each day with a positive expectancy.

2. A right mental attitude is having a proper understanding of the problems you face, their source, and knowing how to approach them with God's Word. You need to know your enemy and how he operates. You need to know his weaknesses. I'll tell you two of them:

    (1) He cannot stand PRAISE; and

    (2) He cannot stand the WORD OF GOD!

    He has no refuge from them. He has to flee from them. He cannot tolerate either.

3. A right mental attitude enables you to possess peace, calmness, self-control and the determination to win no matter how difficult your situation may seem.

4. A right mental attitude demands that you drive out all negatives from your consciousness and focus on God's Word.

REJOICE! FOR THIS IS THE WILL OF GOD CONCERNING YOU!

Everywhere you look these days, people are hurting. They're getting desperate to hear from God, and to know His will for their lives. Are you one of those people? If so - get ready. I'm going to tell you God's will for you right now in the midst of the trouble, heartache, or whatever trial you're facing: *Rejoice evermore. Pray without ceasing. In every thing give thanks: for this is the will of God in Christ Jesus concerning you* (I Thessalonians 5:16-18).

That's it! That's the will of God for you. "Oh no, Brother! You don't understand. I need to know if God wants me to change jobs; who I should marry; if I'm called into the ministry..." Hold on! If you're not willing to obey

Today's Scripture

My brethren, count it all joy when ye fall into divers temptations.

James 1:2

the instructions God has already given you, how are you ever going to hear more? You have to start with what you know. He didn't say to rejoice evermore if everything is working out, or pray without ceasing if every time you pray, you see instant results, or give thanks if you're not going through anything bad.

He said give thanks **in** everything, not **for** everything. There's a difference. You don't thank God **for** trials. You thank God **in** trials. It doesn't matter how bad your circumstances are, you have reason to rejoice, and I'm going to show you why.

The first reason you don't have to worry about your situation is this: **God is faithful!** He will not permit you to undergo any test beyond your endurance. Whatever crisis there may be in your life, before it ever came, God made sure you would be able to endure it. If God thinks you are able to endure it, then it's time for you to line up your thinking with His. Why even consider defeat if God has already equipped you to win? There are people who have gone through exactly what you're going through right now, and made it through victoriously... *so can you*!

Here's another reason you can rejoice: God has promised that with every temptation, He will make *a way of escape*! This means that trials and "escape-ways" are inseparable. But the Devil doesn't want you to know it. That's why every time you're going through a test, he keeps telling you, "There's no way!" I learned a long time ago, when the Devil keeps pressuring me with that, it's always an indication that "the way" is about to be revealed.

The problem with most of us is we get tunnel-visioned; so focused on the trials, that we quit looking for a way out. All we do is talk about the trial. We need to do exactly what God says. **Rejoice!** Why does He want us to rejoice? The joy of the Lord is your strength! If you don't have joy, you won't have strength.

Joy comes from the Word. You have to read the Word constantly to have joy. You may sleep and slumber, but the Devil won't. The moment you open your eyes, he'll say, "You're not going to make it. This trial is going to kill you!" But the Devil doesn't have any defense against joy.

Let me tell you what it means to *rejoice*. One meaning of the Hebrew word **rejoice** is *to brighten up*. Put a big smile on your face. Another meaning is *to spin around*. A third meaning is *to leap*. So, the next time you're in a trial, here's the way you're going to respond: smile, spin, and leap!!

"I thought I needed faith to get through these problems." You do! Faith is like dynamite. It will blow your mountain of problems into the sea. But, JOY is the fuse that ignites it! So, go ahead, light that fuse!

ARE YOU FED UP?

Are you faced with situations that cause you to shout, "ENOUGH IS ENOUGH!"? Are you getting fed up with the enemy causing havoc in your life? Casting the care of your problems over on the Lord and not taking them back is one of the **hardest things to do.** Especially when the cares involve situations that face you twenty-four hours a day! Some problems never seem to go away.

In I Peter 5:6-7, we see these instructions: *Humble yourselves therefore under the mighty hand of God, that he may **exalt you in due time**: Casting all your care upon him: for he careth for you.* Do you see that if you do not cast your cares on Him, you may not be exalted above your circumstances or problems?

Today's Scripture

Humble yourselves therefore under the mighty hand of God, that he may exalt you in due time: Casting all your care upon him; for he careth for you.

I Peter 5:6-7

The Bible says that the Devil is seeking *whom he may devour*. He seeks to devour you by getting you to take on the care and pressure of your situation so that you are consumed with it. When you do cast your care on the Lord, it looses the power of God to work in, and through, the situation and allows Him to bring miracles and victory.

One of Satan's mightiest forms of deception is through *subtlety*. He uses subtlety to steal our blessings and keep us from receiving God's best. *Subtlety* means the enemy catches you *unaware*. His devices can be so highly camouflaged that you do not even notice what is happening. If your blessing has been taken away from you, then find out where the door was opened to the subtlety of the enemy and **shut that door**! Most of the time I have found that my mouth had something to do with it.

God is not saying for us to pretend the problems don't exist, but He doesn't want us to **take on the care**. To take on the care means that you are constantly **talking** about the problem, **thinking** about the problem, **worried** about the problem, and in your mind, there doesn't appear to be any way out! You may think you are trusting God, but you have literally tied God's hands.

It's like saying, "If I can't handle this situation - neither can God." If you don't, at some point, cast the care over on the Lord, then you prolong the "due time." Remember that you are not in an isolated situation. You are not the only one going through what you're going through - even though it feels like your problems far exceed anyone else's.

Genesis 27:40 (*New International Version*) says, ...*when you grow restless, you will throw his yoke from off your neck.* When you finally get fed up with constantly battling things in your life, you will throw his yoke from off your neck! The *Living Bible* says, *Yours will be no life of ease and luxury, but you shall hew your way with your sword.*

It is not going to be comfortable, but if you want this yoke off your neck, you will have to hew your way with your sword. What is your sword? The Word of God!

When problems hit your life, that is not the time to give up! The question is, can you last until the "turning point" comes? You have to! Verse 40 continues, ...*for a time you will serve... but you will finally shake loose from him and be free.*

When you and I get fed up, restless in our spirit, and we begin to walk in our dominion and hew our way with our sword, then God causes the anointing to come on the scene. And, THE ANOINTING DESTROYS THE YOKE OF BONDAGE!

The Word of God is not a defensive weapon; it is an offensive weapon; it is to attack with! You have to reach the point where you literally get "fed up" down on the inside, and you grow restless over what is happening to you. **Enough is enough**! Victory will come as you use your offensive spiritual weapon - **the Word of God**!

NO TURNING BACK

I have found, in times of pressure and persecution, that it is easy to see where Christians really stand with the Lord. I want to encourage you that whatever might come in the days ahead, to make the decision that you're in this to stay! You have to decide that there is NO TURNING BACK!

You're not in this just as long as everybody loves you. In fact, if the world loves you, you've got problems. Jesus said, "If you love me the world will hate you." If everybody in town is in love with you, then you're **compromising** somewhere.

Once you make Jesus the Lord of your life, there's nothing back there for you.

Today's Scripture

Preach the word; be instant in season, out of season; reprove, rebuke, exhort with all longsuffering and doctrine. For the time will come when they will not endure sound doctrine; but after their own lusts shall they heap to themselves teachers, having itching ears; And they shall turn away their ears from the truth, and shall be turned unto fables.

II Timothy 4:2-4

Everything you desire is ahead of you, not behind you. The world does not have what you're looking for. If it did, you would never have come to Jesus.

You and I are living in a time when things are getting very sticky. Satan realizes that his days are numbered. He realizes that Jesus will return soon, which means he doesn't have much time to work.

It's time for the Body of Christ to grow up. It's time for us to become mature and make up our minds once and for all, "As for me and my house, we will serve the Lord!" If you have made the decision to put God first place in your life, to seek first the kingdom of God and His righteousness, then Jesus says you can't look back. You can't keep one eye on the world and one eye on God. You can't straddle the fence. In fact, the Bible says that God is a jealous God. He will not accept a divided heart from His people.

The closer we get to the appearing of the Lord Jesus Christ, the more intense the attacks will become. At the same time, if we have our eyes on Jesus, and our hearts full of God's Word, then we're not going to grow weaker as the attacks intensify, but stronger. **Major attacks will bring major victories!**

Jesus is not coming for a Church that is beat up, worn out, and half-dead. He's coming for a glorious and powerful Church. It will be a Church that is devastating Satan's camp and taking back what he has stolen from us. If the persecution is increasing, then rejoice! That just means the day is getting closer!

Notice what Jesus said about Paul at the beginning of his ministry to Ananias: ...*Go thy way: for he is a chosen vessel unto me... For I will show him how great things he must suffer for my name's sake* (Acts 9:15-16). The suffering Jesus was talking about was persecution. Even though Paul knew he would suffer from the very beginning, he put his hand to the plow and didn't look back.

At the end of his ministry, he could say: *I have fought a good fight, I have finished my course, I have kept the faith* (II Timothy 4:7). Paul is not boasting here but is simply saying, "I've been through many things for Jesus, but I've finished the course. I've kept the faith." You can sum all that up in four little words, "I HAVE NO REGRETS!"

You may not be at the end of your journey as Paul was, but you still may experience pressure and persecution. Don't consider looking back, but keep your hand to the plow. Make up your mind that you are going to go forward, no matter what comes against you. Then you'll be able to say, **"I didn't turn back. I have no regrets!!"**

VICTORY AND SUCCESS ARE YOURS!

The Word of God is spiritual law. God's Word tells us how to achieve success in Joshua 1:8 *(Amplified): This Book of the Law shall not depart out of your mouth, but you shall meditate on it day and night, that you may observe and do according to all that is written in it. For then you shall make your way prosperous, and then you shall deal wisely and have good success.*

The spiritual law involved in this verse is this: **Talking the Word + Meditating the Word + Acting on the Word = Prosperity, Success, and Dealing Wisely.**

I have applied this spiritual law to my personal life and ministry, and it has brought

Today's Scripture

This book of the law shall not depart out of thy mouth; but thou shalt meditate therein day and night, that thou mayest observe to do according to all that is written therein: for then thou shalt make thy way prosperous, and then thou shalt have good success.

Joshua 1:8

great results. I want to share with you **four prerequisites to victory:**

1. **DECISION**: Make a decision to win. The Spirit of God said this to me: "Son, if you are not willing to make a decision to win, then you are not going to win." Success begins with your decision to succeed.

2. **DETERMINATION**: Be determined to back your decision to win. Many people make a decision to succeed without being determined and usually give up under pressure. Once you decide to win, then you must make an unwavering commitment to keep going forward.

3. **DISCIPLINE**: Discipline yourself to **do** only what the Word says and to **say** only what the Word says about **every** situation. You cannot be moved by what you see, feel, or hear.

4. **DILIGENCE**: Always make a steady, consistent effort to accomplish your goal. Never give up!

   Do you need a miracle? Make your **decision** now to get it! Be **determined** that you will win! **Discipline** yourself to think, speak, and do only what the Word says. Be **Diligent**! Never give up! Once you have done these things, **victory and success are yours**!

THE FORCES OF LIFE

Many Christians are crying out for more faith, love, and power; but God has already given us these things. The problem has been that many people have just let these forces of life lie dormant. God has given us these forces (or fruit) designed to work in our lives and produce great results. It is like a guy who has a million dollars in the bank and never learns how to write a check. He is living in poverty, not being able to take advantage of his resources.

The Bible says that God has already caused the love of God to be shed abroad in our hearts by the Holy Ghost. Where is God going to get any more love? He has filled us with Himself, and the Bible says that God is love.

Today's Scripture

Consider it wholly joyful, my brethren, whenever you are enveloped in or encounter trials of any sort or fall into various temptations.

James 1:2 - Amplified

There are people who pray for more faith. The Bible says that God has dealt to every man the measure of faith. We have received faith the moment we were born again.

In Proverbs, we see that we are to protect our spirit. It says to keep your heart with all **diligence**. It did not say to be a lazy Christian. I have seen many lazy Christians who are mad at the ones winning. They have the same potential that any of us have, but the difference between us is that we tap into our potential, and they don't.

It makes no difference to God where you came from, what your name is, or your background. He doesn't have one child in His family who was born a loser. **every** child of God is a potential winner.

If God has given us the potential to win, how do we tap into it? The Bible is not a "you ought to" book, but it is a "here's how you do it" book. Proverbs 4:23 says, *Keep thy heart with all diligence. Diligence* is a word that many people do not like because it means work. You'll work much harder when you start living by faith, but you'll also find that you are headed for the greatest adventure of your life.

Proverbs 4:23 goes on to say, *...out of it* (the heart or spirit) *are the issues of life.* Another translation says, *Protect thy spirit with all diligence, for out of your spirit flow the forces of life.*

Look at Galatians 5:22-23: *But the fruit* (or the forces) *of the Spirit is love, joy, peace, longsuffering, gentleness, goodness, faith, meekness, temperance: against such there is no law.*

Love is a powerful force. The Bible says that the love of God never fails. The flesh wants to retaliate, but if you let the force of love flow out of you, you will always come out the winner. Love is already dwelling in you, but you need to learn how to tap into it. It is an act of your will.

The Bible says that God is LONG suffering. If He wasn't, He would have given up on us a long time ago. We have blown it so many times, but God is LONG suffering. The Bible says that we are partakers of His divine nature; therefore, we should be men and women of patience.

The force of joy is very powerful. It is the **thrust** behind faith. The Bible tells us to count it all joy when we fall into divers temptations. He is saying that the force of joy will really pay off when you are under pressure. Yes, that is the hardest time to have joy, but just try it. You'll see. The devil hates it when he comes against you with a trial, and you have joy during it. **You cannot be defeated** when the force of JOY is being released in your life.

Every one of these fruit are spiritual forces, and they reside in you. You do not have to pray for them, they are already yours. You have to tap into them. You have to learn how to exercise them and release them. The Word of God develops these forces. Don't let the forces of life lie dormant in your life - BE DILIGENT!

THE WAY OF FAITH

There are rewards for walking in the ways of God. But, in order to **walk** in His ways, you need to **know** His ways. There are five basic categories of the ways of God in the New Testament:

1. Walk in faith

2. Walk in love

3. Walk in light

4. Walk in the Spirit

5. Walk in fellowship

I really want to concentrate on the **way of faith**. Blessed is the man that walks in the

Today's Scripture

But this thing commanded I them, saying, Obey my voice, and I will be your God, and ye shall be my people: and walk ye in all the ways that I have commanded you, that it may be well unto you. But they hearkened not, nor inclined their ear, but walked in the counsels and in the imagination of their evil heart, and went backward, and not forward.

Jeremiah 7:23-24

ways of the Lord! One benefit of walking in the ways of God is that you will **prosper** in all you do. If you walk in the counsel of the ungodly, you will be **compromising**. What is compromise? One definition is *spiritual erosion*. It is the erosion of good intentions.

No one sets out deliberately to compromise. All of us have good intentions where the Word is concerned. We hear the Word and decide to walk in it, but sometimes our good intentions are eroded.

The way of faith causes you to go **forward** in life. The way of compromise causes you to go **backwards**. The way of faith enables you to remain patient and endure to the end - cleaving to, trusting in, and relying upon God to see you through. Those who have chosen the way of compromise end up drawing back, quitting, and turning their backs on God's Word.

The way of compromise "seems right" and "appears straight," but notice the outcome is **defeat and destruction**. It produces undesirable fruit in one's life, and it always appears to be justifiable. Jesus illustrates in His teachings that to choose the way of compromise is to choose the way of the **fool**, and to choose the way of faith is to choose the way of the **wise**.

WHICH WAY HAVE YOU CHOSEN?

The only way you can go forward in a world that is going backwards is to walk in the ways of God! Walk by faith and not by sight. Even though it seems that the way of faith is the "hard way," it is the way to victory! Even though standing in faith takes longer sometimes, it is God's way. It will have lasting rewards! **Choose the way of faith!**

FAITH FOR TODAY

In order to overcome today's pressures, you will have to walk by faith. I, personally, would not want to be living in this decade without knowing Jesus, and having a firm grip on the Word of God. It is the Word of God that makes the difference in our lives. Life is hard, but can you imagine how hopeless it would seem if you didn't know the truth that sets men free?

God is looking for an army of believers who are consistently walking in the Word. You may be the **only** representation of Jesus that some people see. They need to see people who are stable, joyful, and peaceful. Stability, consistency, and discipline draw people to Christ.

I learned many years ago that faith is

Today's Scripture

Then said Jesus to those Jews which believed on him, If ye continue in my word, then are ye my disciples indeed; And ye shall know the truth, and the truth shall make you free.

John 8:31-32

the victory that overcomes the world (I John 5:4), and it will continue to be the victory that will overcome the world, no matter what kind of perilous times come. For that reason, we must continue to develop our faith and never allow anything or anyone to talk us out of it. **Living by faith is not a movement! It is a lifestyle.**

I see many members of the Body of Christ back in bondage again. Be careful about what you subject yourself to. If any teaching you hear puts you back in bondage, and changes your lifestyle of freedom, you can count on this: what you heard is not of God!

God has imparted truth into your spirit, and you can't let thieves come along and steal it. As you are diligent in the Word, there will be a built-in "security alarm" that goes off when you hear things that aren't true.

What brings freedom? **Truth**. You only know the truth when you continue in the Word. Freedom is an on-going process. Continue in the Word!

It's one thing to never hear the truth. It's another to hear it and let it go. That's miserable. Your spirit will give you no rest and no peace when you know the truth and are not doing it.

Stand fast in what you have learned! Don't let anyone steal it from you! **Go back to the basics**! Remind yourself of the basics of faith and the principles of walking by faith in God's Word DAILY. Don't be moved by what you see or what you hear, but be moved by what you believe - GOD'S WORD! Don't let go of the foundational truths. Continue in what you have learned and **do it**!

WARNINGS AND ADMONITIONS FROM THE HOLY SPIRIT

The Lord instructed me to share these steps with you. I believe they will help keep you stable in times of trouble:

1. **Hear what the Holy Spirit is saying to the Church.**

2. **Set your house in order.** Time is running out.

3. **Realize the seriousness of the hour.** There is no time left for playing church.

4. **Stir yourself up spiritually, and rise above mediocrity.**

Today's Scripture

And if it seem evil unto you to serve the Lord, choose you this day whom ye will serve; whether the gods which your fathers served that were on the other side of the flood, or the gods of the Amorites, in whose land ye dwell: but as for me and my house, we will serve the Lord.

Joshua 24:15

Arise from spiritual slumber and be about the Father's business.

5. **Establish new priorities.** Put God first in **everything** you do. You must decrease so that He will increase. Get out of yourself and into God.

6. **Go back to the basics and learn to worship God daily.** Begin your day with Him. Learn to worship Him before you do anything else. End your day with Him - thanking and praising Him for allowing you to live in this hour when the world will see the manifestations of His power and glory.

7. **Give His Word first place in your life and make it final authority in all the affairs of your life**. Stir up the truths that you have heard and determine to stand on them, no matter what opposition comes your way.

8. **Walk in love and avoid strife at all cost.** Be a peacemaker.

9. **Break away from the crowd.** Dare to be different. Don't let the

world squeeze you into its mold.

10. **Keep your eyes on Jesus.** People come and go, but Jesus will always be the same!

11. **Be consumed with zeal for God.** Do something to promote the Gospel everywhere you go.

12. **Be a soul winner!** He who wins souls is wise.

13. **Give! Give! Give!** Don't ever stop giving!

14. **Get out of debt.** God wants you to be financially free! Determine that you will get control of your finances and get out of debt. Discipline yourself and be diligent about it. Don't waiver in this. Don't over-extend yourself. God wants you free!

Remember this: the next few years will be the most important years of your life. DON'T WASTE THEM! You have the potential to be victorious in all that you set out to do. Put God FIRST!

OUR APPOINTMENT WITH DESTINY

Do you realize that you and I are watching events take place in our world today that were written and declared by men of God centuries ago?

It is obvious that God has His hand upon this planet and from the very beginning of time, He has established an appointment with destiny.

God has already expressed His will for our lives. If you are deeply committed to Him, then your steps are being ordered by Him, and your life will turn out just the way He planned it. Doesn't it bring great comfort to you to know that the One Who created the universe is in charge of **your destiny**?

Today's Scripture

Remember the former things of old: for I am God, and there is none else; I am God, and there is none like me, Declaring the end from the beginning, and from ancient times the things that are not yet done, saying, My counsel shall stand, and I will do all my pleasure.

Isaiah 46:9-10

••

God moved on holy men, our forefathers, in days past and inspired them to speak utterances into this universe. He inspired them to write things about the generations to come. Just think what the odds are of someone prophesying 700 years before the birth of Christ, that He would be born in Bethlehem, and it being fulfilled.

The psalmist, in Psalm 22, prophesied that Jesus' hands and feet would be pierced, signifying crucifixion. This was written by divine inspiration 500 years before crucifixion became a means of execution. God's Word is precise! The Bible gives specific details, and they came to pass just as they were spoken.

Someone once asked me how I could base my life, my success, and my destiny on something men wrote when we know that men are capable of failure. I answered it this way: "Because Jesus did. He based His life and destiny on God's Word spoken through men."

On the Mount of Temptation, when Satan came against Jesus, He did not say, "Get behind me, Satan, because I am the Son of God." He based overcoming that temptation on something men wrote, inspired by the Holy Spirit. Jesus said, "It is written..." He believed that what Moses wrote was accurate and precise, and He based His success on it.

If Jesus trusted in what Moses wrote under the inspiration of God, then we can trust what Peter, John, or James said. We can know that they spoke under the inspiration of God, and their words will cause us to overcome as well.

God wants us to have hope for the future. He wants us to know that no matter what Satan attempts, God is still in control. He has a wonderful future planned for us.

We must not allow adversity to destroy our hope for the future. If we'll be patient, and remain uncompromising, God promises that His plans for our lives will come to pass. Keep your expectancy high today, and even though the world is in turmoil, have hope for the future.

SEVEN STEPS TO A SCRIPTURAL FOUNDATION FOR HEALING

Today's Scripture

1. **Know that it is God's will to heal you.**

    The Bible declares that it is the will of God that all men be saved and come to the knowledge of the truth. It also says that He not only forgives your iniquities, but He heals all your diseases. It was the will of God that Jesus die at Calvary as our substitute. He bore our sickness and disease so we do not have to bear it now (Isaiah 53:3-10).

2. **Recognize sickness and disease as the work of Satan.**

    Jesus healed all that were oppressed of the Devil. The Bible does not say He

He is despised and rejected of men; a man of sorrows, and acquainted with grief: ...Surely he hath borne our griefs, and carried our sorrows: ... But he was wounded for our transgressions, he was bruised for our iniquities: the chastisement of our peace was upon him; and with his stripes we are healed.

Isaiah 53:3-5

healed all that were oppressed of God. Sickness is bondage from the Devil; it is captivity. Jesus doesn't have to use sickness and disease to teach us. Christ has redeemed us from the curse of the law. Therefore, I am redeemed from sickness (Galatians 3:13).

3. **Realize that healing begins within.**

You must see yourself healed on the inside before you will be healed on the outside. It is not enough to have hands laid on you, and expect somebody else's faith to do all the work. Allow the Word to form an image of divine health in your spirit first, then your body will respond (Proverbs 14:30).

4. **Establish a point of contact.**

A point of contact will help you release your faith. The moment you say, "By His stripes I am healed," that is your point of contact. Once you establish your point of contact, then stand on it until the manifestation comes (Mark 5:28).

5. **Do not wait for "some day" to release your faith. Release it now!**

   Faith is now, not in the future. Today is the day for deliverance, healing, preservation, prosperity, safety, and soundness. Reach out and take what belongs to you right now (Hebrews 11:1).

6. **Shut the door on defeat!**

   The moment you establish your point of contact and release your faith, you shut the door on the enemy. You must refuse to talk defeat and sickness. Do not talk about what you feel, but what you believe. Stand guard over your mouth (Ephesians 4:27).

7. **Place yourself in an environment of faith.**

   When you stand on the Word of God, the Devil will try to fill you with doubt and unbelief. Stay in the Word, then an environment of faith will be created around you (Romans 10:17).

HEALING FOR WOUNDED FAMILIES

I don't know what you are going through in your marriage and family relationships, but the Holy Spirit does. The first step to recovery or deliverance in any area is to be willing to admit that you've made a mistake. It is very easy to place the blame elsewhere, but we must take responsibility for our actions and admit our mistakes. Others can be at fault as well, but before the healing can come, we must be willing to admit we are part of the problem.

Sometimes it's easier to back away than to make relationships work. There may be misunderstandings and situations that arise beyond our control. However, if we desire to make the relationship last, it will take **patience**,

Today's Scripture

Love bears up under anything and everything that comes, is ever ready to believe the best of every person, its hopes are fadeless under all circumstances, and it endures everything [without weakening].

I Corinthians 13:7 Amplified

understanding, and **tolerance**. But it will be worth all the effort.

Hurt feelings cause people to withdraw, usually from those who love them the most. Offenses occur through harsh words, bitter statements, unfair criticism, or because of short-tempers or insensitivity. If our manner offends, we must be willing to change and others should be willing to give us time to change.

Many times people are unwilling to forgive and restore relationships because of selfishness. Sometimes our flesh enjoys carrying something as far as it will go. But healing can come if there is a willingness to obey the Word of God.

Conflicts can only be resolved by understanding the true meaning of love. We have the ability to love like Jesus loved and forgive like Jesus forgave. Quarrels, misunderstandings, and disputes can't mend themselves. Time doesn't heal all. It takes the Word of God. Forgiveness must happen before these hurts can be forgotten.

STEPS IN RESTORING A BROKEN RELATIONSHIP:

1. Determine the **source** of the problem (Hebrews 12:14-15). Some conflicts erupt due to: harsh words, insensitivity, neglect, too much talking and not enough listening, and/or indifference.

2. Determine to **restore** (Matthew 5:9). Be willing to initiate the restoration, no matter who is at fault. YOU take the responsibility.

3. Determine to **forgive** (Ephesians 4:31-32).

4. Determine to be **patient** (Hebrews 10:35-36).

It can take time for trust to rebuild, so don't give up. Restoration will come! Read I Corinthians 13:4-8 for today's scripture, and where you see the word "love," insert your name because that kind of love is in you. (I suggest the Amplified version.)

THE UNCOMPROMISINGLY RIGHTEOUS

The reality of righteousness is definitely a key to victorious living, for the Word of God states in Romans 5:17 *(Amplified Bible)*, *...those who receive God's overflowing grace and the free gift of righteousness reign as kings in life...*

We are to reign in this life as kings instead of life reigning over us. We have been made the righteousness of God and because of this, we are guaranteed success. Many people have said, "Well, I know that I am the righteousness of God, but I'm not successful." The problem here is that this person has never made a quality decision to win. As the pressures of the enemy come, they always give up and quit. You must realize this fact - **failures**

Today's Scripture

Awake to righteousness, and sin not; for some have not the knowledge of God: I speak this to your shame.

I Corinthians 15:34

are not God made! If you follow God's instructions, you will win!

As you awake to your right-standing with God, then sin becomes a thing of the past. The greater the revelation of righteousness, the less sin occurs in your life. The word *sin* just simply means *to miss the mark*. When you sin, you miss the mark for God's best in your life.

The sin most committed by Christians is not murder, adultery, or stealing, but **compromise**. So many miss the mark because they refuse to stand strong on the Word. When pressure comes, they look for an avenue to compromise.

Compromise usually occurs when you have done all to stand, and it appears that nothing is working. You should realize that, at this point, you have the best opportunity to lean hard on your right-standing with God. This is where you can excel and rise above the problems and difficult circumstances in your life.

I believe the following Scriptures will be most rewarding for you, if you'll begin to make them a daily confession. As you confess them, it will build a new awareness of your right-standing with God, and the fact that you don't have to be beaten any longer, for you are **the uncompromisingly righteous**!

Proverbs 10:3 *(Amplified Bible)* says, *The Lord will not allow the [uncompromisingly] righteous to famish...*

Proverbs 10:6 *(Amplified Bible)* says, *Blessings are upon the head of the [uncompromisingly] righteous...*

Psalm 34:19 *(Amplified Bible)* says, *Many evils confront the [consistently] righteous, but the Lord delivers him out of them all.*

Psalm 37:25 *(Amplified Bible)* says, *I have been young and now am old, yet have I not seen the [uncompromisingly] righteous forsaken nor his seed begging bread.*

Psalm 37:39 *(Amplified Bible)* says, *But the salvation of the [consistently] righteous is of the Lord; He is their Refuge and secure Stronghold in the time of trouble.*

As you read these Scriptures, you will note that God intends for you to win. How? By taking an uncompromising stand on your rights as a child of God. God will back you!

ABUNDANTLY INCREASING IN GOD'S DIVINE FAVOR

Today's Scripture

Hear instruction, and be wise, and refuse it not. Blessed is the man that heareth me, watching daily at my gates, waiting at the posts of my doors. For whoso findeth me findeth life, and shall obtain favour of the Lord.

Proverbs 8:33-35

What is *favor*? It is something granted out of good will. You can't really earn it. It's just the goodness of God. It's the fact that God is so merciful and loving that He wants to grant you a favor.

Another definition is: *a gift bestowed as a token of regard*. In other words, God just wants you to know how much regard He has for you, so He does favors for you as a token. The Bible says that the Lord is merciful, gracious and full of compassion. The Hebrew translation of **compassion** is *disposed to show favors*!

I don't think we have believed God for favor like we should. We are always asking people, "Would you do a favor for me?" Or, "Could you do me a favor?" God is disposed to show favors TO US!

When the favor of God goes before you, it opens doors that **no** man can shut! It opens doors that men say are impossible to open! The favor of God will change rules, regulations, policies, and even bring down governments, if necessary, to get you through the door God wants you through.

The favor of God will work for you not only in spiritual things, and not only in life and death situations, but the favor of God will go before you and cause the very desires of your heart to come to pass. If you are up against battles right now and you have done everything you know to do, and you're not getting anywhere, then call on the favor of God! Say, "God, I need a favor!"

The favor of God on your life enables you to win battles that are impossible for you to win in your own strength. Psalm 5:12 says, *For thou, Lord, wilt bless the righteous; with favor wilt thou compass him as with a shield.*

When the favor of God is upon you, you can walk with your head held up high even in life's storms, because somehow - some way, you know the favor of

God will take care of it and turn it into a **victory**! Confess this every day over your life: "My Covenant calls for an abundant increase of the favor of God in my life!"

YOU ARE SOMEBODY SPECIAL TO GOD!

You are so special to God. In fact, you are His treasure! He considers you the most valuable of all His creations. In Psalm 8:3-5, the Psalmist is reflecting on the greatness of God and writes, *When I consider thy heavens, the work of thy fingers, the moon and the stars, which thou hast ordained; What is man that thou art mindful of him? and the son of man, that thou visitest him? For thou hast made him a little lower than the angels, and hast crowned him with glory and honour.*

God has crowned you with glory and honor! YOU are God's prized possession! You are more important than all His handiwork. And you need to see yourself in that light.

Today's Scripture

The Lord bless thee, and keep thee: The Lord make his face shine upon thee, and be gracious unto thee: The Lord lift up his countenance upon thee, and give thee peace.

Numbers 6:24–26

You are not that old man anymore if you are born again. The very divine nature of God is within you and the blood of Jesus flows in your veins! You are of a royal family in the spirit realm! You have a crown on you that can't be seen with the natural eye, but you can walk in that honor because you are highly favored by God.

There are some people who do not receive victories in their lives because of such low self-esteem. Jesus said that we are to love one another as we love ourselves. There are people who hate themselves and hate their lives. They don't like anything about themselves. How will they love someone else?

A low self-esteem is a result of a lack of knowledge. But when you know you have been crowned with glory and honor, then confidence will spring up in your inner man, and you will have the courage to face anything. Many Christians are living way below their privileges because they don't know that they are highly favored of God. So, they don't expect good things to happen.

Revelation knowledge will cause you to see yourself the way God sees you - crowned with glory and honor! He sees you highly favored and successful in everything you set your hand to do. When you truly believe that God has crowned you with glory and honor, you will take authority over adverse circumstances in your life and expect God to turn adversity into victory!

Doubt and insecurity will vanish as you become more and more conscious of God's favor in your life.

In John 12:26 we read, *If any man serve me, let him follow me; and where I am, there shall also my servant be: if any man serve me, him will my Father honour.* If you have chosen to serve Jesus - then the Father will honor you.

Expect victory in every situation simply because you know that you are the object of God's affection. Receive God's love for you and see yourself as His prized-treasure - because you are!

To order related material, call, write or visit our website for further information.

Jerry Savelle Ministries International
P.O. Box 748
Crowley, TX 76036
817/297-3155
www.jsmi.org

Dr. Jerry Savelle is a noted author, evangelist, pastor and teacher who travels extensively throughout the United States, Canada, and around the globe. He is president of Jerry Savelle Ministries International, a ministry of many outreaches devoted to meeting the needs of believers all over the world.

Well-known for his balanced Biblical teaching, Dr. Savelle has conducted seminars, crusades and conventions for over thirty years as well as ministering in thousands of churches and fellowships. He is in great demand today because of his inspiring message of victory and faith and his vivid, and often humorous, illustrations from the Bible. He teaches the uncompromising Word of God with a power and an authority that is exciting, but with a love that delivers the message directly to the spirit man.

In addition to his international headquarters in Crowley, Texas, Dr. Savelle is also founder of JSMI-United Kingdom, JSMI-South Africa, JSMI-Asia, JSMI-Tanzania and JSMI-Australia. In 1994, he established the Heritage of Faith Bible Institute and School of World Evangelism. It is a two-year school for the preparation of ministers to take the Gospel of Jesus Christ to the nations of the world. He also has a Bible School in the U.K. and more recently started a church in Crowley, Texas, called Heritage of Faith Christian Center.

The missions outreaches of his ministry extend to over 50 countries around the world.

Dr. Savelle has authored many books and has an extensive video and cassette teaching tape ministry and a nation-wide television broadcast. Thousands of books, tapes, and videos are distributed around the world every year through Jerry Savelle Ministries International.

.NOTES.

.NOTES.

NOTES

.NOTES.